31 DAYS OF
GOD'S PROMISES

ALPHA BOOK PUBLISHING

ALPHA BOOK PUBLISHING
4132 E. Joppa Rd. Suite 1123
Notthingham MD, 21236

ISBN 978-0-9997159-6-3

TABLE OF CONTENTS

DAY 1

GETTING TO THE HEART OF THE MATTER

"by which have been given to us exceedingly great and precious promises, that through these you may be partakers of the divine nature, having escaped the corruption that is in the world through lust."
2 Peter 1:4NKJV

When standing on the promises of God, we must get to the true heart of the matter. This truth that must be unveiled is how much the Father loves you. His unfailing love grants you access to the exceedingly great and precious promises of God. You must have a clear understanding that God wants to give you the desires of your heart because of the unceasing love he has for his children. You should know beyond a shadow of a doubt that God loves you. Therefore, you can stand on his words. "Delight thyself in the Lord, and he shall give thee the desires of thine heart." Psalms 37:4

- God has promised that those who believe in Jesus and are baptized for the forgiveness of sins will be saved. (Read Mark 16:16 and Acts 2:38).
- God has promised that all things work together for good to those who love and serve Him faithfully (Romans 8:28).

Question to Ponder: Have you ever questioned the love God has for you due to past sins or regrets?

_____

_____

1

Thoughts

_____

_____

_____

_____

_____

_____

_____

_____

_____

_____

_____

_____

_____

_____

_____

_____

_____

_____

_____

_____

_____

_____

_____

Thoughts

DAY 2
HE IS AN ABSOLUTE GOD

"For with God nothing will be impossible."
Luke 1:37 NKJV

When we say that God is Absolute, we mean that He is the ultimate or supreme being. With this knowledge, we must start each day with the expectation of greatness. This expectation comes from serving a great God that cannot fail. He has the power to accomplish whatever promises he desires. The fulfillment of promises is based on his knowledge, power, and timing. God can occupy any space and time. He is all-knowing and all-powerful. When your faith is wavering, you deny the power of the Absolute God. When you find yourself up against great challenges and find it hard to see the light of day, always remember that Man's extremity is God's opportunity!

- God has promised to supply every need we have. (Philippians 4:19)
- God has promised us the power to get wealth that He may establish His covenant which He swore to your fathers, as *it is* this day. (Deuteronomy 8:18)

Question to Ponder: Is there anything too hard for the Lord?

_____

_____

_____

Thoughts

_____

_____

_____

_____

_____

_____

_____

_____

_____

_____

_____

_____

_____

_____

_____

_____

_____

_____

_____

_____

_____

_____

Thoughts

_____
_____
_____
_____
_____
_____
_____
_____
_____
_____
_____
_____
_____
_____
_____
_____
_____
_____
_____
_____
_____
_____

DAY 3
I AM THE PROMISE

God is not human, that he should lie, not a human being, that he should change his mind. Does he speak and then not act? Does he promise and not fulfill?
Numbers 23:19 NIV

The promises of God are more than materialistic gain, fame, or fortune. You are a part of the promises of God. He wants to rescue us from the pain of this world. He made a promise over 2 thousand years ago that he would return for the believers in Christ. Many are experiencing rejection, abandonment, and significant disappointments in life. This too shall pass. God has made a promise while at Calvary that he would remember us. A promise remains how Jesus will return as the bridegroom, and we will be the bride. The blowing of the trumpet shall sound, Jesus will appear in the clouds, and take His church to heaven. In whom ye also trusted, after that, ye heard the word of truth, the gospel of your salvation: in whom also after that ye believed, ye were sealed with that holy spirit of promise. Ephesians 1:3 KJV

- God promised that He would deliver us from this present evil world, according to the will of God and our Father. (Galatians 1:4)
- God promised to go and prepare a place for you; he will come again and receive you to himself; that where He is there, you may also be. (John 14:3)

Question to Ponder: Is the Rapture a truly comforting thought?

_____

_____

Thoughts

Thoughts

_____

_____

_____

_____

_____

_____

_____

_____

_____

_____

_____

_____

_____

_____

_____

_____

_____

_____

_____

_____

_____

_____

_____

DAY 4
A Promise in the Sky

"For all the promises of God in him are yea and
in him Amen, unto the glory of God by us."
2 Corinthians 1:20 KJV

Often right after a storm on a summer day, you can look up in the sky and see a rainbow. On rare occasions, you may see a double rainbow. The bible mentions the blessings of the rainbow during at least three occasions. In the book of Genesis, the rainbow can be viewed directly after the great flood. It is considered a symbol of God's covenant with the Earth and mankind. Ezekiel used the rainbow as a comparison to the magnificent glory of God. Lastly, Revelations mentions how the rainbow was around the throne to signify the power of God's throne. When you are in the storms of life remember the blessings that come from the covenant made with the rainbow. If you are favored to see the double rainbow, you can expect the double promise. The Father wants you to receive a double portion of his blessings. For no matter how many promises God has made, they are *"Yes"* in Christ. And so through him, the *"Amen"* is spoken by us to the glory of God.

- God promised to give you plans for good and not for disaster, to give you a future and a hope. (Jeremiah 29:11)
- God promised that you shall not perish but have eternal life when you believe in him. (John 3:16)

Question to Ponder: What indications have God revealed to you that he would fulfill your promise?

_____

_____

Thoughts

_____

_____

_____

_____

_____

_____

_____

_____

_____

_____

_____

_____

_____

_____

_____

_____

_____

_____

_____

Thoughts

_____

_____

_____

_____

_____

_____

_____

_____

_____

_____

_____

_____

_____

_____

_____

_____

_____

_____

_____

_____

_____

_____

DAY 5
PROMISED LAND

But he brought us out from there to bring us in and give us
the land he promised on oath to our ancestors.
Deuteronomy 6:23

New land is a promise that was given first to your ancestors, and now you must believe that it is promised to you. This Land can be physically or spiritually received. God will bring you out of bondage into a land of freedom. Be careful to follow every command the Lord has given you today so that you can live and increase and may enter and possess the land the Lord promised in Deuteronomy 8:1 (NIV). God wants to bring increase to your life through the acquisition of real estate and property. If you carefully obey his instructions, you can increase greatly in a land that is rich and flowing with milk and honey.

- God promised to give you every place that the sole of your foot shall tread upon. (Joshua 1:3)
- God promised that you might go and takeover the good land when you do what is right in the Lord's sight. (Deuteronomy 6:18)

Question to Ponder: Do you believe that every place you set your foot, the land can be yours?

_____

_____

_____

Thoughts

_____
_____
_____
_____
_____
_____
_____
_____
_____
_____
_____
_____
_____
_____
_____
_____
_____
_____
_____
_____
_____
_____

Thoughts

_____

_____

_____

_____

_____

_____

_____

_____

_____

_____

_____

_____

_____

_____

_____

_____

_____

_____

_____

_____

_____

DAY 6

Lift Up a Shout of Victory

*One of you routs a thousand, because the LORD your
God fights for you, just as he promised.*
Joshua 23:10

God is worthy of all the glory and praise because he has won the
battle just for you. You may be battling cancer, depression, or
diabetes but God has already won the fight. Lift up a shout of
victory for the battle is won. Lift up your heads and allow the
king of glory to come in. Tell the spirit of defeat to leave because
you are victorious. Your God is fighting for you. He is working
behind the scenes even when it feels that things are getting
worse. You are greater than your problem ad greater than your
pain. Victory belongs to you because you are one with the Him.
"But thanks be to God, which giveth us the victory through our
Lord Jesus Christ." 1 Corinthians 15:57 KJV

- God promised that you have overcome them because
  greater is he that is in you, than he that is in the world.
  (1 John 4:4)
- God promised we are more than conquerors through
  him that loves us. (Romans 8:37)

Question to Ponder: When you go to war against your trials
and tribulations, do you use your own strength, or do you
access and operate in God's strength?

_____

_____

_____

16

Thoughts

_____

_____

_____

_____

_____

_____

_____

_____

_____

_____

_____

_____

_____

_____

_____

_____

_____

_____

_____

_____

Thoughts

DAY 7

The Ultimate Defender

Defend my cause and redeem me; preserve
my life according to your promise.
Psalm 119:154 KJV

The universal declaration of Human Rights states that anyone who stands trial is innocent until proven guilty. Somehow, many Christians continue to be persecuted just because of their belief in the one true God. Often, they are tried for the sins of their forefathers and attacked for standing up for holiness. Through it all, salvation is for the righteous and God will protect you through your trial and tribulation. He will cover you from the hands of the enemy and strengthen you when you feel like giving up. Just as the job of the defense attorney is to protect the client, God is your defender, and you will have the victory. "For the promise, that he should be the heir of the world, was not to Abraham, or to his seed, through the law, but through the righteousness of faith." Romans 4:13 KJV

- God promised to be my strong tower and very present help in the time of need. (Proverbs 18:10)
- God promised that we might be made the righteousness of God, for he hath made him be sin for us, who knew no sin. (2 Corinthians 5:21KJV)

Question to Ponder: What trials are you facing that you need God to defend and strengthen you on?

_____

_____

_____

19

Thoughts

_____

_____

_____

_____

_____

_____

_____

_____

_____

_____

_____

_____

_____

_____

_____

_____

_____

_____

_____

_____

_____

Thoughts

DAY 8
HIS BANNER OF LOVE COVERS ME

He brought me to the banqueting house,
and his banner over me was love.
Song of Solomon 2:4

The swelling motions of the ocean are filled with billows of waves. Just when you think the wave has washed ashore another one is swiftly approaching. God's love is so compelling it can be compared to the billowing waves in the sea. Right when you think his love is fading, He reminds you of his everlasting love. His love becomes a standard against self-defeat, self-righteousness, and self-doubt. God's love is a gift that will never vanish. It is not based on gender, race, or creed. His banner is wide enough to cover as many who desires to access it. When the banner is applied over your life, no weapon, word, or attack that is formed against you can succeed.

- God promised to be my Banner. (Exodus 17:15-16)
- God promised to give those who fear him a banner that will be displayed. (Psalm 60:4)

Question to Ponder: How do you envision God's Banner of Love?

_____

_____

_____

Thoughts

Thoughts

_____
_____
_____
_____
_____
_____
_____
_____
_____
_____
_____
_____
_____
_____
_____
_____
_____
_____
_____
_____
_____
_____

DAY 9

WISDOM SEEKERS

*For this cause we also, since the day we heard it, do not
cease to pray for you, and to desire that ye might be
filled with the knowledge of his will in all wisdom and
spiritual understanding.*
Colossians 1:9 KJV

The Lord is full of wisdom, and he freely shares it with
whomever he chooses. You must earnestly desire wisdom just
as you need the oxygen you breathe. Come to a place that you
cannot live without wisdom. It's needed to raise a family, be in
good health, and obtain a prosperous future just to name a few
benefits. Most importantly, wisdom allows you to gain access
to the hidden mysteries of Christ. Many are spiritually blind,
but wisdom helps you to see the things of God. Once you come
to know the Love of Christ, you will be filled with the fullness
of God. You will be able to comprehend the breadth, length,
depth, and height of Christ. Remember, God is capable of
doing far more above all we think. (Ephesians 18-20)

- God promised you could obtain wisdom through the
  fear of the Lord. (Proverbs 1:7)
- God promised to give wisdom, and out of his mouth
  cometh knowledge and understanding. (Proverbs 2:6)

Question to Ponder: What are some differences between the
wisdom of man and the wisdom of God?

_____

_____

_____

Thoughts

Thoughts

_____

_____

_____

_____

_____

_____

_____

_____

_____

_____

_____

_____

_____

_____

_____

_____

_____

_____

_____

_____

_____

_____

DAY 10
LONG LIFE

With long life will I satisfy him,
and shew him my salvation.
Psalm 91:16 KJV

Long life is a gift from the Lord. When we think of all the senseless killings and premature deaths in the land, we begin to question this promise. Through obedience to God and following the leading of the Holy Spirit, you do not have to fear death. You can live a long, fulfilling and prosperous life. God has not given us over to a spirit of fear. We have the power over death and can decree life to the fullest.

- God promised we could be in good health even as our soul prospers. (3 John 1:2)
- God promised that we shall live and declare the works of the Lord. (Psalm 118:17)

Question to Ponder: Do you believe that it is God's will that you live a long and prosperous life?

_____

_____

_____

Thoughts

Thoughts

_____

_____

_____

_____

_____

_____

_____

_____

_____

_____

_____

_____

_____

_____

_____

_____

_____

_____

_____

_____

_____

_____

_____

DAY 11

A WINDFALL OF BLESSINGS

For God's gifts and his call are irrevocable.
Romans 11:29 KJV

Windfall blessings are unexpected blessings that are blown down by God. Have great expectations that while you are praying, God has already blessed you. Expect a fresh wind of the breath of God to hit your household. You will have nothing lacking or broken in your life. Decree the Deuteronomy 28 blessing over your life. During the good times and the bad continue to stand on these promises. All these blessings shall overtake you at once when you obey the voice of God. The Lord shall command the blessings upon thee, your storehouse, and your land.

Question to Ponder: Do people see you as blessed?

_____

_____

_____

- God promised you shall be blesses in the city and the field. (Deuteronomy 28:3)
- God promised you shall be blessed when you come and when you go out. (Deuteronomy 28:6)

Thoughts

Thoughts

DAY 12

HEALING WATERS

And so after waiting patiently,
Abraham received what was promised.
Hebrew 6:15 KJV

Healing is the children's bread. If you earnestly desire healing it can be manifested in your life today. Pray that your faith to see healing manifested is made stronger. Walk on the waters as Peter did and receive your healing. Don't look down when the symptoms are still present. Look up and walk it out without being defeated by your sickness and pain. Our healing was paid for on the cross when Jesus received His stripes. "Who His self-bare our sins in his own body on the tree, that we, being dead to sins, should live unto righteousness, by whose stripes ye are healed" (1 Peter 2:24).

Question to Ponder: Can you recall a time you petitioned God for healing, and it happened?

_____

_____

_____

- God promised that we are healed with his stripes. (Isaiah 53:5)
- God promised that we could cast out the spirits with his word and all who are sick will be healed. (Matthew 8:16-17)

Thoughts

_____

_____

_____

_____

_____

_____

_____

_____

_____

_____

_____

_____

_____

_____

_____

_____

_____

_____

_____

_____

_____

Thoughts

_____

_____

_____

_____

_____

_____

_____

_____

_____

_____

_____

_____

_____

_____

_____

_____

_____

_____

_____

_____

_____

_____

DAY 13
SEEING THE IMPOSSIBLE

For truly I tell you, many prophets and righteous people longed to see what you see but did not see it, and to hear what you hear but did not hear it.
Matthew 13:17 KJV

The world is vastly changing, and many are rarely seeing the miracles of Christ. There is great news for those who believe. Miracles, sights, and wonders are still happening today. For with God nothing shall be impossible (Luke 1:37). It is only through faith in God that you can see what is impossible to man, but possible with God. Our God is a great God who heals the Land, restores the broken-hearted, and revives the lost. He is the same God who parted the red sea, delivered Daniel from the lion's den, and allowed the three Hebrew boys to come out of the fiery furnace unharmed. To see the impossible, you must change how you perceive miracles.

- God promised that with Him everything is possible. (Matthew 19:26)
- God promised that his power is made perfect in weakness. (2 Corinthians 12:9)

Question to Ponder: Do you ever feel like you don't have enough faith to believe in miracles?

_____

_____

_____

Thoughts

Thoughts

DAY 14
CHANGING SEASONS

And this is what he promised us- eternal life.
1 John 2:25 KJV

God wants his people to bear good fruit upon the Earth. Our fruit can only be produced during times of prayer and impartation by the Holy Spirit. Just like various fruits can only be harvested in certain seasons, it's the same in our spiritual life. Seasons change and the fruit we bear must change with the season. There are times we are full of faith and times when we are faithless. There are times when we are filled with confidence and other times we lack self-esteem. For everything, there is a season and a time for every matter under the heaven (Ecclesiastes 3:1). It's not for you to know the times and season that the Father has fixed by his authority (Acts 1:7).

- God promised to guard your hearts and minds in Christ Jesus. (Philippians 4:7)
- God promised the earth would remain seed time and harvest, cold and heat, summer and winter, day and night and it shall not cease. (Genesis 8:22).

Question to Ponder: What season are you in?

_____

_____

_____

Thoughts

_____
_____
_____
_____
_____
_____
_____
_____
_____
_____
_____
_____
_____
_____
_____
_____
_____
_____
_____
_____
_____
_____

Thoughts

DAY 15

HEAL OUR LAND

If my people, who are called by my name will humble
themselves and pray and seek my face and turn from
their wicked ways, then I will heal their land.
2 Chronicles 7:14KJV

All throughout the land people are marching for justice. Many groups that are advocating for change have one thing in common; they are all tired of the wickedness in the land. God gave us the solution to the problem decades ago. It is only through prayer and true repentance that we can begin to see our land healed. Financial and natural resources will only create a temporary fix to the problem. Walking around demonstrating gives you a voice in the earth but we need a voice in the heavens to reach God. The time has come for us to sound the alarm and blow our voices in the kingdom. God is waiting on the effectual prayers of those who truly repented to get his attention so he can truly heal our land. Tarry for the power of the Holy Ghost to come down and make this land healed and whole.

- God promised that those who believe shall lay hands on the sick, and they shall recover. (Mark 16:18)
- God promised when we humble ourselves, seek His face and turn from our wicked ways that He would forgive us and heal our land. (2 Chronicles 7:14)

Question to Ponder: What areas do you perceive require the most healing in our land?

_____

_____

Thoughts

Thoughts

DAY 16
REVIVE US AGAIN OH LORD!

After two days he will revive us; on the third day, he will
restore us that we may live in his presence.
Hosea 6:2 KJV

Can these dry bones live again? Can these dry bones dance again, can theses dry bones speak again? Prophesy to these dry bones and say "O ye dry bones, hear the word of the Lord" (Ezekiel 37:4). Sometimes we can start to back pedal while walking in our salvation. We start to have familiar thoughts, feelings, and emotions that we have already been delivered from. Therefore, we must continue to ask God to revive us again oh Lord. Allow God to reveal any iniquities in your heart on a daily basis before you slide backward in your Christian walk. If you confess your sins and truly turn away, you can avoid becoming a walking set of dry bones. Prayer causes the flesh to remain in tack and prevent us from living in the valley of dry bones.

- God promised to save all who confess with thy mouth and believe in thine heart that he was raised from the dead. Romans (10:9)
- God promised to heal (physically, emotionally & physically) those who confess their faults one to another and pray for one another. (James 5:16)

Question to Ponder: Are you living in the valley, when God ordained you to live on the mountain top?

_____

_____

_____

Thoughts

Thoughts

DAY 17
LEVELING THE MOUNTAIN

*I go before you and will level the mountains; I will break
down gates of bronze and cut through bars of iron.*
Isaiah 45:2 KJV

Mountains can become barriers to your destination. God has
ordained greatness for our life, but it does not come without
obstacles. Without faith, you cannot speak to the mountain
that stands between you and your destiny. You must build
yourself up in the Holy faith to level the mountain and live
the abundant life God has designed for you. Mountains of
trials and tribulations are created to stand in your way. When
you think about the formation of a mountain, it is created
from tectonic plates in volcanoes which erupt. When things
start to explode and become rough, take a step back because
you know God is placing a challenge before you. You have
the power and the authority to speak to the mountain and
cast it into the sea by its roots. You no longer need to feel
intimidated by your mountain. Your words carry the power
of the kingdom of God.

- God promised if you say unto the mountain be
  removed and shall not doubt, but believe, you shall
  have whatsoever you say. (Mark 11:23).
- God promised whatever you bind and loose on earth
  shall be bound and loosed in heaven. (Matthew 18:18)

Question to Ponder: What kind of Mountain barriers are you
commanding to be leveled?

_____

_____

Thoughts

Thoughts

_____

_____

_____

_____

_____

_____

_____

_____

_____

_____

_____

_____

_____

_____

_____

_____

_____

_____

_____

_____

DAY 18
GOD'S DOING A NEW THING

"See, I am doing a new thing! Now it springs up;
do you not perceive it? I am making a way in the
wilderness and streams in the wasteland."
Isaiah 43:19 NIV

God is doing a new and awesome thing in your life. A *suddenly* has happened in your life. It only takes one encounter for this new change to manifest in your life. There was a man named Saul who enjoyed persecuting Christians until one day he had a *suddenly*. Saul had a Damascus road experience when suddenly a light from heaven flashed around him. He could no longer stand. After falling to the ground, he heard something new. It was the voice of God questioning his actions. Immediately, Saul's life was changed.

- God promised the good work he began in you would carry on to completion. (Philippians 1:6)
- God promised to cause your new thing to spring up. (Isaiah 43:19)

Question to Ponder: What new things would you like for God to manifest in your life?

_____

_____

_____

Thoughts

_____

_____

_____

_____

_____

_____

_____

_____

_____

_____

_____

_____

_____

_____

_____

_____

_____

_____

_____

_____

Thoughts

DAY 19

The Lord our Redeemer

*He redeemed us in order that the blessing given to
Abraham might come to the Gentiles through Christ Jesus,
so that by faith we might receive the promise of the Spirit.*
Galatians 3:14 KJV

Our Redeemer, the Lord Almighty is his name, the holy one of
Israel. As the Redeemer, he has redeemed you from the curse
of the land. He paid the ultimate sacrifice once and for all
while on the cross. We are no longer under the law but under
the grace of God. Job was stricken with sickness and
persecution, yet he declared, "I know my Redeemer lives" (see
Job 19:25). The Lord is our savior and our redeemer. He
continues to carry our griefs and sorrows. It is through his
love we have been redeemed. Jesus, who is the son of man
gave his life for a ransom to become the Redeemer of the
world. He takes away the sin of the world and reconciles us
back to right standing with God. God wants to redeem us and
make us pure for good works.

Question to Ponder: Can God redeem your time?

_____

_____

_____

- God promised we could obtain eternal redemption by
  his blood. (Hebrew 9:12)
- God promised to redeem us from all iniquity. (Titus
  2:14)

Thoughts

Thoughts

DAY 20

COME HOLY SPIRIT

And I will ask the Father, and he will give you another
advocate to help you and be with you forever.
John 14:16 KJV

God has sent us help with handling the present problems of this world. We grieve the Holy Spirit when we fail to summon his assistance with matters. God gave us the Holy Spirit who is the third person of the Trinity to be a helper. The advocate is available to all who receive him and is baptized with the Holy Ghost. You no longer have to handle problems alone. Satan, who knows his time is limited, wants the children of God to feel isolated. "But the comforter, which is the Holy Ghost, whom the Father will send in his name, shall teach you all things, and bring all things to your remembrance" (John 14:26).

- God promised to seal you with the Holy Spirit unto the day of redemption. (Ephesians 4:30)
- God promised you shall receive power after the Holy Ghost has come upon you. (Acts 1:8).

Question to Ponder: Do you seek the guidance of the Holy Spirit to help you navigate through the issues of life?

_____

_____

_____

Thoughts

_____

_____

_____

_____

_____

_____

_____

_____

_____

_____

_____

_____

_____

_____

_____

_____

_____

_____

_____

_____

_____

_____

Thoughts

_____
_____
_____
_____
_____
_____
_____
_____
_____
_____
_____
_____
_____
_____
_____
_____
_____
_____
_____
_____
_____

DAY 21
POWER OF AGREEMENT

Set his seal of ownership on us, and put his spirit in our hearts as a deposit, guaranteeing what is to come.
2 Corinthians 1:22 KJV

There is power in being properly aligned with God. You must trust his holy words without negotiating or wavering. Praying an agreement prayer can cause breakthrough to happen in your life. What made the Acts 2 encounter so powerful wasn't the words that were prayed but the corporate prayer of agreement. God loves unity and wants his children to lift up their voices with one sound. He desires for his children to be on one accord to release the power of the Holy Spirit. Nations collapse when they are divided. Families suffer when there is divorce. You must realize you can shake the heavens and the earth when you lift up your voices in agreement.

- God promised when two of you agree on earth they can ask and it shall be done. (Matt 18:19)
- God promised to rescue those who are in disobedient when you strive together in prayer. (Romans 15:30-31).

Question to Ponder: Do you have an agreement partner to pray with?

_____

_____

_____

Thoughts

Thoughts

DAY 22
BIRTHING PURPOSE

And by Faith, even Sarah, who was past childbearing age was enabled to bear children because she considered him faithful who had made the promise.
Hebrews 11:11 KJV

Many have joined the rat race to birth new visions and ministries. The competitive spirit has taken off at a rapid pace. Many refuse to look up to the heavens for ministry design. They have neglected the vertical directions for horizontal views. When God is ready to birth your purpose, you must set your affection on things above, not on things on the earth. We cannot trust the opinions of ungodly men to increase our riches. We must hear the word of the Lord to know what he has promised us. In due season you shall reap if you do not faint. Sarah was past childbearing age, but she held on to the promise. You may think you have missed your appointed time to be launched out into the deep, but you are right where God wants you.

Question to Ponder: What stage of the birthing process are you in?

_____

_____

_____

- God promised to give you a heart that knows that he is Lord. (Jeremiah 24:7)
- God promised you are not born of corruptible seed but incorruptible. (1 Peter 1:23)

Thoughts

_____

_____

_____

_____

_____

_____

_____

_____

_____

_____

_____

_____

_____

_____

_____

_____

_____

_____

_____

_____

_____

Thoughts

DAY 23
GRACE TO BE FEARLESS

Now I am about to go the way of all the earth. You know with all your heart and soul that not one of all the good promises the Lord your God gave you has failed. Every promise has been fulfilled; not one has failed.
Joshua 23:14 KJV

When you think of fear, some may think of the cowardly lion from the Wizard of Oz, How can a brave lion be afraid of creatures beneath him in the hierarchy when God made him be above and not beneath? The spirit of fear has the power to paralyze your thinking. God has called you to be fearless and step out of your comfort zone. He has your back, and instead of being like the lion, you must walk in confidence. The Lord, your God, will make you the leader among the nations and not a follower. You will always prosper and never fail if you obey all his commands that he is giving you today (see Deuteronomy 28:13). Have the confidence and grace to be a fearless winner.

- God has promised you victory over the enemy and all of his wicked schemes. (Ephesians 6:11)
- God promised to be the author of your eternal salvation to all who obey. (Hebrew 5:8-9)

Question to Ponder: What area of your life have you allowed fear to take over and prevent you from winning?

_____

_____

_____

Thoughts

Thoughts

DAY 24
SEEKING THE FACE OF THE KING

Now Lord God, let your promise to my father David be
confirmed, for you have made me king over a people
who are as numerous as the dust of the earth.
2 Chronicles 1:9 KJV

To seek the face of the King is to seek the presence of God. You must be intentional when pressing into God and accessing his throne. Ezekiel was able to experience the throne of God and Moses wanted to see the face of God as a representation of endearment. Approaching the throne of a king was one of Esther's most powerful experiences. Before going to the lord with your list or agenda, try accessing the presence of God with worship. You simply cannot approach a king without kneeling in his presence. You must humble yourself before him, and he will welcome you in.

- God promised all these things shall be added to you when you seek first the kingdom of God. (Matthew 6:33)
- God promised that He would be found those who seek Him with all their heart. (Jeremiah 29:13)

Question to Ponder: Have you entered the throne room of God during prayer?

_____

_____

_____

Thoughts

_____

_____

_____

_____

_____

_____

_____

_____

_____

_____

_____

_____

_____

_____

_____

_____

_____

_____

_____

_____

_____

Thoughts

DAY 25

My Heart is Ready to Receive Your Promise

Then they believed his promises and sang his praise.
Psalms 106:12 KJV

How often do we forget God's words concerning the promises he has made to us. The Israelites constantly forgot the promises that were made to them in the Old Testament; the promise to deliver them from the Egyptians, the promise to make them the head and not the tail, the promise to be lenders and not borrowers, and so many other promises. It's interesting how easy one can slide in to sin when we neglect to think about how faithful God has remained in our lives. Get ready to receive something that you have never received by meditating day in the night on the blessings of God. Be ready to receive what God has for you. The promises of God are waiting for you right now.

- God promised to fix our heart as we sing and give God praises. (Psalms 57:7)
- God promised to put understanding in our hearts. (Job 38:36)

Question to Ponder: Is your heart open to receive the promises of God?

_____

_____

_____

Thoughts

Thoughts

DAY 26
TRUSTING THE PROCESS

*For if the inheritance depends on the law, then it no
longer depends on the promise, but God in his grace
gave it to Abraham through a promise.*
Galatians 3:18 KJV

You may have heard stories of relatives who pass away and
leave a monetary inheritance to the family. Sometimes the
inheritance is left without the love one's knowledge. This
could be due to estranged or long distant relationships. The
estranged relationship could create a little tension or
discouragement when it's time to claim the inheritance if a
solid relationship was never built. Guilt can immediately creep
into the situation and possibly a feeling of not deserving the
inheritance. It can be assumed the family member offered
grace due to the fact the loved one was included. God has an
inheritance for us because we are his children. We may not
always deserve God's blessings or promise, but God freely
gives us his grace because we are joint heirs with him.

- God promised we are joint heirs with Christ. (Romans 8:16)
- God promised we are a His children by faith. Galatians 3:26)

Question to Ponder: Do you feel that you are worthy of God's
promises?

_____

_____

_____

Thoughts

_____

_____

_____

_____

_____

_____

_____

_____

_____

_____

_____

_____

_____

_____

_____

_____

_____

_____

_____

_____

Thoughts

_____

_____

_____

_____

_____

_____

_____

_____

_____

_____

_____

_____

_____

_____

_____

_____

_____

_____

_____

_____

_____

_____

DAY 27

TRUE REST COMES FROM ABOVE

*Therefore, since the promise of entering his rest still
stands, let us be careful that none of you be found to
have fallen short of it.*
Hebrews 4:1 KJV

God promised that you should enter into divine rest. Search for this rest that allows you to live for the Lord without growing weary. Build upon your foundations of faith by first honoring the Sabbath. Keep the Sabbath day holy by appreciating the creator and all of his beauty. Resting is a way of submitting to the will of the Lord. Be fervent and apply yourself to a day of both spiritual and physical rest. Find a special time to cease from your labor and spend time at the feet of Jesus.

- God promised to give you rest on every side when you seek God eagerly. (2 Chronicles 15:15).
- God promised to sustain you when you lie down and sleep. (Psalm 4:8)

Question to Ponder: How often do you observe the Sabbath?

_____

_____

_____

Thoughts

Thoughts

DAY 28

LEANING NOT TO MY UNDERSTANDING

*Trust in the LORD with all thine heart, and lean not
unto thine own understanding. In all thy ways
acknowledge him, and he shall direct thy paths.
Proverbs 3:5-6 KJV*

Our ways are not like God's ways, and our thoughts are not
like his thoughts. Therefore, lean not to your understanding.
The natural man has a difficult time receiving the things of the
spirit. The spiritual things of God are foolishness to man. Ask
God to increase your spiritual discernment so that you can
build upon your intimacy with God. The boy Samuel could
not discern the voice of God due to the limited time he spent
in the presence of God. Eli mentored Samuel on how to know
the true voice of God. Follow the voice of the Father and he
will teach you how to drown out the voices that will lead you
astray.

- God promised to help those who are being tempted.
  (Hebrews 2:18)
- God promised not to allow you to be tempted beyond
  what you can bear. (1 Corinthians 10:13)

Question to Ponder: How often do you hear God speak?

_____

_____

_____

Thoughts

Thoughts

DAY 29
DETOUR!

When God made his promise to Abraham, since there was no one greater for him to swear by, he swore by himself.
Hebrews 6:13 KJV

If you think you can help God out with your promises stop dead in your tracks. You are heading in the wrong direction. Using your might, knowledge, or will to accomplish the works of the Lord will lead you down the wrong path. There is no one greater than Elohim. He is the king of glory and the Lord of hosts. He is the creator of all living things and steward over your soul. Therefore, he does not need our help. There is no other name higher than his name. Do not become anxious and allow your heart to turn to another way or stray into other paths.

- God promised to give you many years in the land when you listen to his voice and hold fast to him. (Deuteronomy 30:20)
- God promised to guard our hearts and minds when we submit everything to him in prayer. (Philippians 4:6-7).

Question to Ponder: How strong is your faith in the Lord in times of great adversity?

_____

_____

_____

Thoughts

_____

_____

_____

_____

_____

_____

_____

_____

_____

_____

_____

_____

_____

_____

_____

_____

_____

_____

_____

_____

Thoughts

DAY 30
GUARANTEED PROMISES

Therefore, the promise comes by faith, so that it may be by grace and may be guaranteed to all Abraham's offspring.
Romans 4:16 KJV

The promises of God are an assurance that what He has spoken will be fulfilled. Some lenders in the business sector require some promises to be written in the form of a promissory note or personal guarantee. This powerful guarantee of payment is often used in protecting the business's financial interest. You can discover various men and women of God in the holy scriptures that have proven God to be a guarantee of his word. Your Heavenly Father will never deceive you nor betray you. You can depend on him. God cannot lie nor can his word return to Him void. If God spoke it to you, it is a guaranteed promise.

- God promised that He would always be truthful. (Numbers 23:19)
- God promised to be the fulfiller of the promise (2 Corinthians 1:20)

Question to Ponder: Have you ever wondered if God would fulfill a promise to you?

_____

_____

_____

Thoughts

Thoughts

DAY 31
PROMISE KEEPER

Not one of all the Lord's good promises
to Israel failed; every one was fulfilled.
Joshua 21:45 KJV

Our God is so faithful. He honors his promises, and we should worship the promise keeper for all that he has done both past, present, and future. It doesn't matter how long you have to wait or how many times it falls through. It should not concern you how many times you hear the word no or see someone laughing at you. Stay committed to honoring God. Continue to live a life of fasting and prayer. Humble yourself and become obedient unto death (Philippians 2:8). Wait patiently on the Lord for the promise to be fulfilled. Don't grow weary in well doing, for you will reap at the proper time if you do not give up. (Galatians 6:9)

Question to Ponder: How long are you willing to wait for your promise?

_____

_____

_____

- God promised that you shall be blessed and divinely favored as you fear and worship Him in obedience. (Psalms 128:4)
- God promised to give strength to the weary and increases the power of the weak. (Isaiah 40:29)

91

Thoughts

Thoughts

Made in the USA
Middletown, DE
30 June 2018

31 DAYS OF GOD'S PROMISES

Life can be tough. When the going gets tough, the tough go to the WORD OF GOD. The word of God is faithful and true. The Bible contains the promises of God that you can stand on in any situation that life throws your way.

This book, *31 DAYS OF GOD'S PROMISES*, is a devotional that takes you through a month's journey to learning several promises that God has made to you in the Holy Scriptures. Read them, speak them over your life in faith, and received the blessings of Lord!

ISBN 9780999715963

9 780999 715963

90000